D0882751

Manatees

Precious McKenzie

EYE to EYE
with Endangered Species

ROURKE PUBLISHING
Vero Beach, Florida 32964

© 2010 Rourke Publishing LLC

All rights reserved. No part of this book may be reproduced or utilized in any form or by any means, electronic or mechanical including photocopying, recording, or by any information storage and retrieval system without permission in writing from the publisher.

www.rourkepublishing.com

PHOTO CREDITS: Title Page: © Chris Pollack; 2, 3: © Stacey Lynn Brown; 4, 5, 14, 15: © Amanda Cotton; 6, 7, 12, 13, 18, 19, 20, 21: © David Freund; 7: © Ron Masessa; 8, 9: © Steffen Foerster; 10, 11: © William Attard McCarthy; 12, 13 © U.S. Fish and Wildlife Service; 14: © Jason Register; 16,17: © Andrew Smith; 18,19 © Lindsay Dean; 21: © Chief Mass Communication Specialist Michael W. Pendergrass, © United States Senate, Save the Manatee Club; 22: © Michael Meyer; 23: © Eline Spek; 24: © Lawrence Phillips

Editor: Jeanne Sturm

Cover design by Teri Intzegian
Page design by Heather Botto

Library of Congress Cataloging-in-Publication Data

McKenzie, Precious.
  Manatees / Precious McKenzie.
       p. cm. -- (Eye to eye with endangered species)
  Includes bibliographical references and index.
  ISBN 978-1-60694-403-5 (alk. paper)
  ISBN 978-1-60694-842-2 (soft cover)
  1. Manatees--Juvenile literature. I. Title.
  QL737.S63M37 2010
  599.55--dc22
                                                2009006011

Printed in the USA

CG/CG

ROURKE PUBLISHING

www.rourkepublishing.com - rourke@rourkepublishing.com
Post Office Box 643328 Vero Beach, Florida 32964

Table of Contents

Mermaid?

Early sailors reported sighting creatures that appeared to be part fish, part woman. Sailors called these creatures sirens or, more commonly, mermaids. The sailors believed that mermaids would enchant them with their songs and beauty, causing their ships to wreck.

What the sailors probably saw were manatees.

There are several different **species** of manatees. Scientists have identified the West Amazonian manatee, the dugong, the West African manatee, the West Indian manatee, and the now **extinct** Steller's sea cow. The manatee found in North America is the West Indian manatee.

A manatee will cruise slowly along the river bottom seeking food.

Do We Look Like Mermaids?

Manatees are large **aquatic** mammals. The average length of an adult manatee is between 9 and 10 feet (2.7 to 3 meters) long. Adult manatees weigh between 800 and 1,300 pounds (about 360 to 600 kilograms).

Manatees have unusual faces. Their faces are wrinkled. They have a whiskered, **prehensile** upper lip. This large upper lip functions much like an elephant's trunk. A manatee will use it to uproot sea grasses. A manatee has lungs and nostrils. It needs to surface for air every 3 to 5 minutes.

Marine mammals, including manatees, whales, and dolphins, come to the surface to breathe air, while fish get their oxygen from the water.

Fun Fact

Manatees do not have front teeth. They chew aquatic plants with molars.

Manatees do not have arms or legs. Instead, they have a large, paddle-shaped tail and two front flippers. They use their tails and flippers to help them swim through the water. Manatees are not speedy swimmers. A manatee's highest speed is only 5 miles per hour (8 kilometers per hour).

A manatee uses its tail and front flippers to move about, just as early sailors believed mermaids moved through the water.

Manatee Chatter

Manatees have excellent hearing and can see very well underwater. They communicate with one another through clicks and chirps. Manatee mothers frequently talk to their calves. Scientists have recorded mother manatees vocalizing with their calves and with other adult manatees.

These manatees have algae growing on their backs. Algae grows in moist areas that receive plenty of sunlight. Scientists think algae acts like sunscreen for manatees, protecting them from the Sun's strong ultraviolet rays.

Mothers and Calves

Manatees usually live alone. When they are 5 years old, female manatees are mature and are able to become pregnant. A manatee baby will grow inside of its mother for almost a year. Then the mother manatee will give birth to her baby, called a calf, in the water. A mother manatee will nurse her calf for 1 to 2 years.

Fun Fact

Manatee babies are much larger than human babies. Manatee calves weigh close to 66 pounds (30 kilograms) at birth.

Manatee mothers and calves form loving, close relationships while the calves mature.

Manatee Habitats

Manatees can live in either fresh or salt water. Manatees need warm water in order to survive. If the water temperature drops below 68 degrees Fahrenheit (20 degrees Celsius), manatees cannot thrive.

In North America, manatees prefer the warm waters of the Gulf of Mexico and the Caribbean Sea. They are also found in slow moving rivers, canals, and **estuaries**.

Manatee Habitat Regions

Manatees take short naps throughout the day. Even in their sleep, they rise to the surface for air.

When the water temperature drops in the winter, manatees congregate around the many natural springs in Florida. Springs such as Homosassa or Blue Springs have a constant year round temperature of 72 degrees Fahrenheit (22 degrees Celsius).

Manatees will gather when they find warm water or food, but they are generally solitary animals.

Fun Fact

Manatees enjoy the warm waters surrounding power plants. They are frequently sighted near the power plants in Fort Myers and Apollo Beach, Florida.

Delicious Dinners

Manatees are **herbivores**. They spend 6 to 8 hours a day grazing on sea grasses and plants. Each day manatees will eat 10 to 15 percent of their body weight in aquatic plants. People call manatees sea cows because, like cows, manatees are large and graze on plants.

Manatees eat sea grasses and sea lettuce. An average-sized adult manatee can eat up to 150 pounds (68 kilograms) of underwater vegetation per day.

Saving the Species

In Florida, there are only about 2,300 West Indian manatees, making them an **endangered** species. It is illegal to harm manatees and any person caught harming one could be fined up to $100,000 and sent to prison for up to one year.

They are gentle creatures and pose no threat to humans. Manatees, however, are often injured by boats and jet skis. They have also been crushed by canal locks or flood gates. Many manatees have been injured or killed by fishing nets and fishing hooks. Water **pollution** can make them sick.

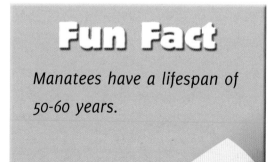

Fun Fact

Manatees have a lifespan of 50-60 years.

In 1981, musician Jimmy Buffett and Florida Senator Bob Graham began the Save the Manatee Club. The Save the Manatee Club educates the public about manatees and **habitat** conservation.

Jimmy Buffett

Bob Graham

Kathleen Phillips volunteers for the Save the Manatee Club. She and her husband, Larry, have adopted a manatee named Robin, one of many available through the Adopt-A-Manatee program.

The United States Fish and Wildlife Service created The Florida Manatee Recovery Plan. This plan protects manatees. There are now speed zones posted in waterways. Boaters must slow down so that manatees can move safely out of the boat's way.

You can help protect the manatee, too. If you see an injured manatee, call 1-888-404-FWCC (3922) or #FWC on your cell phone, or go to VHF, channel 16 on your marine radio. The Manatee Rescue and **Rehabilitation team** will take immediate action to help the manatee.

Glossary

aquatic (uh-KWAT-ik): living in the water

endangered (ehn-DAYN-jurd): a plant or animal that is in danger of becoming extinct

estuaries (ESS-chu-er-ees): the parts of a river where it meets the sea

extinct (ek-STINGKT): a type of animal or plant that no longer exists

habitat (HAB-uh-tat): the natural place where an animal lives

herbivores (HUR-buh-vorz): animals that eat only plants

pollution (puh-LOO-shuhn): materials that contaminate water, soil, or air

prehensile (pree-HEN-sil): made to grasp an object

rehabilitation team (ree-huh-bil-i-TAY-shuhn teem): a group of people who work together to restore an animal's health

species (SPEE-sheez): one specific kind of animal

springs (SPRINGZ): freshwater sources that come from underground

Index

Websites to Visit

kids.nationalgeographic.com/Animals/CreatureFeature/West-indian-manatee
www.savethemanatee.org
www.lowryparkzoo.com/html/l3/fact_sheets/l3_att_hab_fsman_manatee.html

About the Author

Precious McKenzie has loved animals and reading all of her life. She was born in Ohio but has spent most of her life in south Florida, traipsing through the Everglades. Her love of children and literature led her to earn degrees in education and English from the University of South Florida. She currently lives in Florida with her husband and three children.